New England's MAD AND MYSTERIOUS MEN

This book is dedicated to my mad and mysterious friend William "Billy" Cox of Newburyport, Massachusetts, whose resemblance, at least physically, to Timothy Dexter, "The Newburyport Nut," is striking. Billy is an Essex County Court Officer. He is an avid fisherman and he loves to hunt bear. Born on the Fourth of July, he is truly a Yankee-Doodle Dandy, with strong Irish tendencies. He loves dogs, hates kids, and is celebrated for his whiskey tenor.

D1556941

Timothy Dexter   Billy Cox

Cover Photos: ISBN-0-916787-03-6

The Wild Men of Borneo and their keeper, photo courtesy of Circus World Museum, Baraboo, Wisconsin — Johnny Appleseed painting, courtesy of John Hancock Mutual Life Insurance Company, Boston, MA — Al Janard tells the story of The Provincetown Phantom — Linc Hawkes of Marblehead and his magic rooster — Governor John Endicott — Billy Cox dressed as the Newburyport Nut — The Nova Scotia Giantess and her husband Mr. Bates and friend, photo courtesy of Circus World Museum — General Tom Thumb, photo courtesy of Desmond Collection, P.T. Barnum Museum, Bridgeport, Conn. — Dead man after flood, photo courtesy of the Library of Congress, Washington, D.C., and Paul Bunyon, painting, courtesy John Hancock Mutual Life Insurance Company, Boston, MA.

The photo of the hermit in the sunglasses, under the cover Legend, taken at Dogtown in Gloucester, MA, is one of the mad and mysterious owners of Chandler-Smith Publishing House.

I
THE DAY THE WORLD ENDED

When will the world end? Will it end? These are the questions that have provoked the minds of philosophers, clergymen and, from time to time, the average man. There have been many false alarms throughout the ages, and New England has had its share of doomsdays. One of the first was on October 21, 1716.

It was a brisk Sunday morning with a bright sun. Most New Englanders were at church listening to lengthy sermons. At 11:00 a.m., a dark cloud formed in the sky blotting out the sun. No one could read his prayer book; candles had to be lit. "It's the end of the World!" cried a few non-churchgoers from the streets, as most of them joined the congregation inside. Many ministers took advantage of the situation to strike fear into their audiences with repentence and judgement day orations. An hour later, however, the sun broke through the mysterious black cloud and all breathed a sigh of relief.

Doomsday did not come again to New England until May 19, 1780 when, as before, the sun rose but was soon blocked out by a cloud. This time, however, the cloud wasn't black, it was brown and colored everything with what one observer called "an earthly brass-like light." There was thunder and lightening but no rain, and at midday complete darkness set in. Throughout New England, keepers closed their shops and children were let out of school to run home in terror. Nathanial Whittaker of the Tabernacle Church in Salem, Massachusetts, called his people to church, only to be harassed by sailors just off a ship at Derby Wharf, who were shouting through the windows, "The day of judgement has come!" Said Reverend Samuel Cole of Boston, "Christians were stirred to activity and non-professors earnestly sought for salvation." Many people crammed the churches and some remained throughout the night, only to be greeted by a bright spring day the next morning.

There was another so called "Yellow Day" on September 6, 1881, when everything in New England took on a copper color. this time it came in the early afternoon of a warm humid day. As one observer commented in a Boston newspaper next day, "The air assumed a dim, brassy hue, and the obscuration was so great that I could not read the newspaper without artificial light; the faces of people were of a light saffron hue, and the grass and foliage had a marked golden tinge . . ."

There were few explanations for these strange phenomenon, but the most popular theory for the yellow days was that a great forest fire somewhere had clouded the sky and blocked out the sun. The panic of the people during these days produced many doomsday prophets who roamed the countryside preaching and asking for handouts. In the early 1800's, one of the most sophisticated prophets was Harriet Livermore, daughter of a Massachusetts Congressman. Miss Livermore made frequent trips to Washington, D.C., embarassing her father as she insisted that the legislature send all American Indians to Jerusalem to witness the second coming of Christ.

Probably the most effective doomsday prophet was a middle-aged Vermont farmer named William Miller. He was born in Pittsfield, Massachusetts in 1782, the first of 16 children. Certainly, during his younger years there was talk of that mysterious black day of 1780. In his early adult life, Miller was not a churchgoer. He was a lieutenant in the Army, stationed at the Canadian border during the War of 1812 and he narrowly escaped death twice while there. He first accidently fell out of a wagon, split open his head and was unconscious for days, suffering from a brain concussion. A few months later, he was stricken with pox. His arm was badly ulcerated from the disease but — only because Miller insisted — the arm was saved from amputation. After these incidents, he became a churchgoer. Miller married Lucy Smith of Poultney, Vermont, where they settled after the War.

In 1816, when Miller was 34 years old, there was another Doomsday — in fact there was a series of them. It wasn't just New England that was affected this time, but 25 states. It began in the Spring when the earth didn't thaw and northern farmers couldn't plant their crops. During May and June they were inundated with hail and sleet storms. There were eight nights of frost in New England during the month of June; Summer temperatures fell to 40 degrees as far south as Florida. The few crops that had been planted in late Spring were ruined. Vermont — where Miller was living — had a severe summer snow storm and it snowed in the Great Lakes region during July. There was no green in New England that Summer; the grass was hay; dead leaves fell from the trees as did thousands of dead birds. Also, a strange halo was arching the sun each day. Many, including William Miller, read and re-read the many prophecies of doom in the Bible. Miller took particular count of the Revelation in the Bible that mentions a change of seasons during "The Last Days." Although scientists concluded that the wintery summer of 1816 was caused by a volcanic eruption in Bali (in the East Indies) carrying a heavy ash over the United States, blocking out the sun's rays, Miller insisted it was a prelude to Judgement day.

He spent over a year trying to mathematically calculate — from Daniel's prophecy and The Revelation — when the world would actually end. He concluded it would be sometime in the year 1834. Miller started hearing voices that told him to "prepare the world for the end." It was 1832 and he was 50 years old, of meager circumstance, and in poor health. There was no way, he thought, that he could tell the people of the world to prepare for the end and even if he could, he had only two years in which to do it. His chance came however, one Sunday morning, when the local church pastor was ill and Miller was called upon to preach at the Dresden, Vermont Baptist Church. His sermon shocked and fascinated the small congregation. "Graves will open up. Christ will reappear. There will be signs in the heavens. The wicked will be defeated by God and they will be cast into hell, while we — the righteous ones — shall live in eternal bliss."

Within two hours, Miller became a prophet. The word spread like wildfire. He was invited to preach by many other Vermont ministers. Soon, Joshua Hines of the Boston Baptist Church heard about Miller. Hines was a promoter who wanted converts. He invited Miller to Boston. The church was packed, and Miller didn't let Hines down. The people left the church terrified and bent on repentance.

Joshua Hines became Miller's John the Baptist, entering one New England town after another, promoting Miller's prophecies before "the Chosen One" arrived to preach. To add impetus to Miller's claim, on November 13, 1833, the sky was showered night and day with falling stars. The shower of stars, some 250,000 of them, continued for hours, lighting the sky above the Boston horizon . . . and some explosions were heard as the stars fell.

"Immediately after the tribulations of those days shall the sun be darkened, and the moon shall not give her light, and the stars shall fall from the heaven, and the powers of the heavens shall be shaken . . ." (Matthew 24:29-30) Miller now had over 50,000 followers.

Not everyone believed Miller. When he began preaching at a church in Newburyport, Massachusetts one evening, a mob threw stones and eggs at him, but Miller kept on talking over the sound of whistles and curses as he ducked flying objects.

His biggest problem was that 1834 came and went, but the world didn't end. Miller announced in January 1835 that his calculations could not be exact, but that the world would surely end by 1843 or 44.

This gave him some ten years to continue preaching his Doomsday prophecy. With the continuous, large contributions he received from "believers," a Judgement Day Tabernacle was built in Boston. Joshua Hines wrote and printed pamphlets about Miller and, although big city newspapers wrote tongue-in-cheek articles about him and Dooms Day, he steadily gained support in the towns. One Boston paper printed an article in 1842 saying that Miller's tabernacle was insured for seven years, yet the world was supposed to end within two.

In April of 1843, a massive comet appeared in the sky. Its tail was 200 million miles long and no one could look up without marveling at its brilliance. It was aptly named "The Great Comet of 1843." Miller, of course, used the comet as a sign of things to come. In January 1844 Miller's followers saw rings around the sun and crosses blazing in the sky. The time had come!

Miller left the tabernacle on March 20 to wait out the end at home. Many of his followers had made white robes in which to ascend to heaven, and some people arrived at the Tabernacle, at town churches, and on country hillsides in the nude. At Salem, Massachusetts a large group of robed Miller followers climbed Gallow's Hill — where the witches had been hanged — to await their judgement. Many went to cemeteries to meet departed friends and relatives "when the graves would open up." One grave-sitter lost his second wife when she departed in a huff because he was waiting for his first wife to reappear.

Probably the greatest panic of Miller followers was at Westford, Massachusetts where some 80 people awaited the end of the world inside a church. A man named Amos Jackson decided to have some fun. He went home, got his bugle, and waited in the bushes outside the church until midnight March 21; then he blew the bugle. People in white robes stumbled out of the church, some falling to their knees, others crying and screaming hysterically. Gabriel had blown his horn! When they spotted old Amos in the bushes, they were furious. "How do," said Amos to Reverend Brown. "When are you and all these people gonna leave us?"

Miller and his followers were, of course, disappointed, and Miller lost the great majority of his Doomsday believers. It was disastrous for many of them, for they had sold homes and farms, or had given them away, and owned nothing but the robes they stood in on March 21, 1844. Miller died a bitter old man years later, deserted by his followers. Fortunately for the rest of us, however, the world went on and will hopefully continue to do so for many years to come.

II
THE NEWBURYPORT NUT

I guess we've all met exceptional men and women in our time, those who seem to shine above others in one way or another. They may have a special personality trait, unique character, special talent, or a touch of genius. Timothy Dexter had none of these, but there is no denying that he was exceptional. His personality was grave, and he hardly ever smiled, yet people thought him funny. He was not a man of character, although he tried diligently to make people think he was. He had no special talent, yet he was successful; and although his business dealings and foresight seemed to border on genius, most people thought he was merely lucky. Indeed, it was phenomenal luck, with maybe a touch of shrewdness and a dash of adventurous spirit, that made Timothy Dexter one of the most unique individuals who ever lived.

He was born in Malden, Massachusetts in 1743. His youth was relatively uneventful, although his parents thought him slightly eccentric even then. He had an obsession to rub shoulders with the great and near-great. He wanted to make history. Although he was from a poor family, Timothy longed to be a member of Boston's high society. He worshipped King George III before the American Revolution and John Hancock after it. His dreams were of wealth and power, even though, until his early twenties, he was but a leather dresser's apprentice in Malden. Saving most of his hard-earned money, and marrying a not-so-fair young maiden who had a sizeable dowry for a farm girl, he moved to Newburyport, a seaport town on the Merrimac River renowned in the Colonies for its wealth and culture.

The gaunt little man opened a shop in Newburyport where he made and sold gloves and garments for men. At the age of 32, when the American Revolution began, he had a tidy savings of gold and silver from his business. His friends thought him mad when he traded in his cash for the depreciating currency offered by the new Continental government. Most people knew that this paper money was near worthless, and men like John Hancock were to lose a fortune on it. Was Dexter a fanatical patriot, or did he forsee something most others could not?

Dexter did admit that he had occasional dreams that foretold the future, and he followed the dictates of these dreams no matter how foolish they seemed to him and others. If it was the sandman who told Dexter to spend his gold on Continental paper currency, then everyone should have such dreams. When Alexander Hamilton instituted his banking and financial reforms after the war, Dexter became a millionaire. He then began to do things which everyone in town thought ridiculous.

With his "tons of silver," as he called it, he bought thousands of pairs of mittens, 42,000 brass warming pans and over 100 crates of live cats. He loaded these items aboard nine sailing vessels at Newburyport, all of which were bound for tropical islands in the West Indies. The sea captains shrugged their shoulders — "What the hell," commented one captain, "Dexter is footing the bill, but what on earth will the plantation owners and natives of the Caribbean do with mittens, warming pans and cats?"

The ship with the mittens aboard met another ship in a southern port that was heading for the Baltic. The mittens were sold to this Baltic trader at a good profit. "The cats sold like hotcakes," Dexter later reported, "to the many West Indian warehouse owners who wanted to rid their storerooms of rats." The warming pans, with their covers removed, brought a 75 percent profit when sold to plantation owners as sugar ladles and molasses strainers. The West Indian natives also used them as frying pans. Dexter had done it again, but he delighted more in the surprise of his Newburyport neighbors than he did in his profits.

The sandman must have whispered in Dexter's ear a few nights after the warming pan coup, for he soon purchased 21,000 Bibles which he also shipped off to the West Indies in 21 ships. With the Bibles went printed notes to all the plantation owners which read: "All of you must have one Bible in each family or you will go to hell." This wasn't a joke. Dexter believed his words, as did the plantation owners; again, Timothy turned a profit. Local merchants, who considered Dexter a gullible braggart, banded together to inform him that he would gain a great profit if he shipped coal to Newcastle, England. The devious merchants, of course, realized that Newcastle was the coal producing capital of England. Timothy, unfortunately, didn't realize this and, following their advice, sent three shiploads of coal across the Atlantic to that city. The ships arrived just as a coal miners' strike got under way, and Newcastle merchants were thrilled at Dexter's foresight. Again, the eccentric little man made a substantial profit.

Now he had more money than he knew what to do with, but Newburyport society would still not accept him. His neighbors considered him odd, crude, and "possibly insane." Dexter's next move didn't help his image, though he thought it would.

He bought a mansion on Newburyport's exclusive High Street. He painted the house white, trimmed with gaudy green, built a cupola on the roof and topped it with a flying golden eagle. He didn't stop there. Wooden statues began appearing on the fence posts and on platforms in the front yard; they were the work of a shipyard carpenter named Wilson. Wilson carved 40 of these statues at $15,000 apiece. Over the main entrance to the mansion were eight-foot tall statues of George Washington, Thomas Jefferson, and John Adams. Scattered about the garden were John Hancock, King George, William Pitt, General Knox, the governors of New Hampshire and Massachusetts, Lord Nelson, Louis XVI, and a few others of Dexter's favorites. He was now surrounded by the great and near-great. It was a display any museum would be proud of, but the Newburyport elite were not impressed. "My house and gardens will make my stuck-up neighbors burst with envy," Dexter told his carpenter. But the neighbors weren't envious.

After years of work on these statues, which included animals, religious leaders, and Indian chiefs, as well as famous men, Wilson became despondent as did the artist who was hired to paint buttons, bows and cheek blush on all of these characters. The reason the artist and carpenter finally left Dexter's employ, even though the pay was phenomenal, was because he would change his mind every day or so. He would want a statue attired in civilian clothes and, when Wilson was almost completed, Dexter would demand the statue wear a military uniform. A statue could be Napoleon one day, and have to be reconstructed or repainted to be General Glover the next day. Dexter also insisted that certain names be spelled incorrectly, which drove the artist to drink. For example, Thomas had to be spelled "Tomas," for what reason, no one knew. Finished or not, the carvings were uniquely grand and people came from miles around to see them and to catch a glimpse of the eccentric who owned them.

Timothy did not like all the visitors who came to gawk at his house, and when he tried to shoo one old man away from his home, the man refused to go. Timothy asked his near-demented son Samuel to shoot the man — surprisingly Samuel refused. Dexter grabbed the gun from Samuel and fired. Luck was with Timothy again, for he missed, but the old man took him to court; the verdict was that Timothy Dexter spend six weeks in the Ipswich Jail.

Not only was the son a problem, but Timothy's wife was troublesome as well. She didn't understand her husband's vanities and obsessions. Even his day-to-day clothing was an embarrasment to her. He'd always wear a cocked hat that was sizes to big for him, silver buckled shoes, frilly shirts, bright colored knickers, black and red coats with silver stars on the collars, and he usually carried a gold cane. He traveled constantly with a mangy little hairless dog named "Pepper," which he coddled in public much to his wife's disgust.

His carriage was as ornamented as his clothing and property. The Dexter coat-of-arms was prominent on the coach doors, but, since the Dexter arms did not have a crest, Timothy made one up. It was a hand holding a warming pan with the motto "By this I Got Ye." The carriage was drawn by two majestic cream colored horses. "Clear the way for Lord Timothy Dexter," the children of Newburyport would shout as the carriage rolled into town. The men would laugh at him and the women would snub him. Timothy didn't like the teasing, laughing and snubs. He even became fearful of the older boys who razzed him unmercifully, so he hired bodyguards for protection. This only added to what was known locally as "Dexter's Circus," for he dressed his guards in silly-looking medieval uniforms.

There were a few local parasites in Newburyport who spent their time flattering Dexter, and some even lived in his mansion. They continuously primed his ego to gain room, board and some spending money. They convinced him that he was the greatest philosopher in the world, and to acclaim this title, he had a lifesized statue carved of himself, holding a sign that was placed on a pedestal at his front door. The sign read: "I am first in the East, first in the West, and the Greatest Philosopher in the World."

Society further shunned him as did his wife, when he wrote, and had printed an autobiography titled, Pickle For The Knowing Ones. Anyone who read the book became thoroughly confused with his philosophy, which was a mixture of religion, voodoo, and business dealings. The book was filled with terrible spelling and had no punctuation marks. At the end of the book he wrote: "Mister printer the nowing ones complane of my book had no stops I put in anuf here and they may peper and salt it as they please." Following, were pages of periods, commas, colons, and question marks.

One of the parasites who lived from time to time at the mansion was a fish peddler named Jonathan Plummer. Dexter thought him a genius, for he was a man who liked to say things in rhyme. Plummer also liked to tell dirty stories in verse. Dexter decided to hire him as his personal poet. "Every day you must write something about me," he told Plummer. After a few months of feeding Dexter's vanity, Plummer went back to selling fish, but in the interim, he wrote this:

"Lord Dexter is a man of fame,
Most celebrated is his name,
More precious far than gold that's pure
Lord Dexter shines forever more!
His house is white and trimmed with green;
For many miles it may be seen;
It shines as bright as any star
The fame of it has spread afar.
Lord Dexter like king Solomon,
Hath gold and silver by the ton;
And bells to churches he hath given
To worship the great King of Heaven."

When Dexter's wife continued to nag him about all the strange people in the house, and the strange figures on the front lawn, he, for awhile, made believe that she was a ghost. He told those around him that she was just an apparition, due to indigestion, and that no one should pay any attention to her jabbering. Finally Dexter decided he could stand her complaining no longer and he offered her $2,000 to leave him. She accepted, and next day he advertised for a new wife in the local newspaper. No one applied so, after a few weeks, he hired his old wife back - but before she would return, she made him give her another $2,000.

His wife had tried to convince him that his friends weren't really loyal and were only befriending him for his money. To prove her wrong, he decided to hold a mock funeral for himself. He made all the preparations and even had a spacious tomb built in the garden of his mansion. He ordered an expensive mahogany coffin trimmed with silver, bought mourning apparel for his friends and family, and sent out invitations to most of the townsfolk. Dexter, of course, wanted to attend the funeral himself to study his friends' reactions to his death, but they convinced him that his presence would not be appropriate, so he watched the proceedings from a second story window in the mansion. Only a few people gathered at the tomb. Most citizens of Newburyport avoiding another of Dexter's follies, but those who attended seemed to be sad enough to satisfy Timothy. Everything was going well until the guests entered the house for refreshments. They discovered Timothy in the kitchen beating his wife because she hadn't shed a tear at his funeral.

A few years later, at age 63, Timothy Dexter really died. He would have rejoiced at the funeral, for thousands attended, including many of

Newburyport's high society. The only problem was that Timothy wanted to be buried in the tomb he had erected in his front yard, but the town fathers, "for sanitary reasons," would not allow it. He was instead buried in the public grounds at Frog Pond.

A hurricane three years later knocked down and destroyed most of the wooden statues surrounding the mansion, and the house itself soon fell into disrepair. It was used as a factory boarding house in 1845, and later owners removed all the ornate carvings. The house remains today, without its embellishments, as one of the many handsome mansions that line Newburyport's High Street.

Timothy Dexter's wish came true. He did make history; not as the greatest philospher in the world, but certainly as one of the strangest men who ever lived in New England.

Timothy Dexter's house on High Street, Newburyport - it stands today without its embellishments. Next door is the Lowell-Johnson House, noted neighbors who shunned Dexter.

III
SALEM' S WILD IRISH ROGUE

On a cold winter evening in 1819, big Michael John Martin was rowed ashore to Derby Wharf in Salem, Massachusetts. He had arrived in port on the brig MARIA out of Waterford, Ireland. Michael was a tall, handsome lad of twenty-five years, with blue eyes, blond hair and a ready smile. He was one of four sons born to a poor farming family of Kilkenney. He immediately found work in Salem as a farm laborer for the wealthy Ezekiel Hersey Derby. Derby himself soon became so fond of the carefree, energetic Michael that he made the young man his personal house servant. Michael, in fact, was liked at once by everyone who met him. Besides being personable and polite, he was a good worker and had super-human strength.

For over a year no one in Salem was wise to the fact that Michael Martin was the infamous "Captain Lightfoot", a legendary highway robber who was a wanted man in Ireland, England and Scotland. He received the name "Captain Lightfoot" in Ireland, where he had been a most polite and gentlemanly thief, constantly eluding capture. He was, in fact, Europe's Public Enemy Number One.

Content with his new friends and position in America, Michael was determined now to lead an honest life, and there were many young girls who would have him settle permanently into the quiet day-to-day life of Salem. Michael, however, also enjoyed Salem's night life and spent most of his evenings carousing at the Sun Tavern on Essex Street, and at the Black Horse Tavern on Boston Street, in Salem's Irish district. It was at the Black Horse that Michael Martin met Asa Doyle, who was later to become Michael's partner in crime. "Martin became intemperate," Ezekiel Derby reported. "I was unable to reason with him and despite a broken heart, I was obliged to dismiss him."

Michael headed for the highway. On his way north, he took up his old profession. Dressed as a priest, he held up two wealthy men on horseback at Beverly, Massachusetts. Besides money, he took one of their horses. At the New Hampshire border, disguised as a Quaker clergyman, he robbed five more riders. He then made his escape into Canada dressed as a woman, riding his stolen horse sidesaddle to Quebec. There, still wearing a dress, woman's wig and makeup, he attended a wedding. At the wedding reception he stole every guest's money and jewels. He did, however, allow the bride to keep her wedding ring. Borrowing another horse, he headed back for the American border.

Before crossing, he waylaid a priest and took his money and his clothes, then re-entered the United States at Vermont — again dressed as a church man.

While eating dinner at a Burlington, Vermont inn, Michael was recognized and had to make a speedy escape into New Hampshire. Laying aside his priestly garments, he then disguised himself as an Indian. Trotting along the highway, naked to the waist, he stopped travelers for handouts of food; then he would take them for everything they had — sometimes leaving them naked to the waist.

Dressed again as a woman — with a bonnet and blonde wig — he entered Boscawen, New Hampshire. Here, for a few days he rode up and down the main roads, nodding and saying "howdoo" to wealthy gentlemen who passed by on horseback. Then he would ride ahead, dismount and stretch out on the road. When the wealthy horsemen came along and bent over the seemingly distressed female, Martin would clout them over the head and take their money.

Returning to Massachusetts, he met up with his Salem friend Asa Doyle again, and together they ventured to Boston on a robbing spree. Attending a parade at Boston Common, Martin and Doyle learned that Governor Brooks was giving an exclusive dinner party that evening at a mansion in Medford. They rode to Medford, hoping to rob some of the dinner guests as they returned from the party. Martin and Doyle spent the remainder of the day drinking at Medford's Jefferson Inn, which was located on the main turnpike. The innkeeper later reported that both men drank an uncommon amount of brandy. "Later," the innkeeper said, "Doyle had no countenance for the deed ahead, and he left my inn, never to return . . .When a gentleman in handsome dress went by the inn," said the innkeeper, "Martin hurried to the stable, mounted his horse and rode after him."

Martin's victim was Major John Bray of Boston. At a secluded section along the Medford Road, he approached the major and commanded him to deliver up his valuables. The major handed over his watch and a purse with $9.00 in it. Martin then wheeled his horse and fled. The major, however, was not one to give up his belongings that easily. Obtaining the help of a few friends, he persued Martin all the way to Springfield, Massachusetts, where they found the highwayman asleep in bed at a local inn.

Michael Martin, alias Captain Lightfoot, was brought back to the East Cambridge jail to await trial. This was the first case to be tried under a new state law — passed only four months earlier by the General

Court — specifying that a convicted highwayman was to receive the penalty of death by hanging. Throughout the proceedings, at which Ezekiel Derby appeared in Michael's behalf, Michael himself was cool and calm, and at times even witty. When the judge pronounced the sentence of death, Michael Martin dryly replied, "Well, that's the worst you can do for me."

During his last few days behind bars, Martin somehow procured a file, presumably from his friend Doyle. He filed off his wrist and ankle chains, and when the prison guard came with his breakfast on the morning of December 8, 1821, Martin struck the man unconscious. He ran into the prison yard that was surrounded by a high wall. The yard gate was made of hard oak and was secured with a padlock. Martin threw himself at the gate four times and succeeded in knocking it down. He started running down the street as the alarm was sounded. He then raced through a cornfield with twenty men chasing him. After running for some 200 yards, three guards caught up with him, but Martin managed to knock each one unconscious. The others then pounced on him, wrestled him to the ground, and he was recaptured.

To the sound of muffled drums, Michael Martin walked from his prison cell to the gallows. Many had come to see him hang— most out of curiosity to see "the merry strongman," who a Boston reporter described as "a perfectly formed man with muscles put together in mighty power."

He smiled at the crowd and even joked with them as he climbed to the platform. Standing beside the gallows were two black horses leading a wagon that contained Michael's coffin. Michael stared at it for a moment, then said to all in attendance, "I have a private carriage to take me into eternity."

As the crowd laughed, the trapdoor fell open and Michael Martin, age twenty-seven, was swinging to and fro, a roguish grin still creasing his face.

IV
MAD DOG McGOVERN

"Old Ironsides" was anchored in Plymouth Harbor, England, surrounded by British warships of all sizes and shapes. Only fifty yards away on her port side was the RAZEE carrying 50 cannons and, next to her, a British black frigate carrying 38 guns. Close by on the CONSTITUTION's starboard side was the notorious sea-warrior POICTIERS, with 78 cannons lining her decks. Isaac Hull, commander of the 44-gun frigate CONSTITUTION, realized that cannons from the shore batteries and surrounding ships were pointed at him, probably over 500 of them. Although America and England were not at war, relations between the two countries were strained to near breaking point — both sides realizing that upon the slightest provocation, war would erupt.

Commodore Hull was reluctant to allow any of his 400 officers and men to go ashore, for the British Navy had no qualms about capturing American sailors on shore-leave, or from defenseless vessels, then forcing them into slave labor aboard their own ships. This shanghaiing of American seamen was to lead both countries into the War of 1812 a few months later. Hull decided to let his men visit Plymouth, but warned them all to beware of British press-gangs — they were to travel in groups of four or more while on shore and to avoid pubs frequented by British sailors.

On the wintery afternoon the CONSTITUTION was to way anchor and head back to home port in Charlestown, Massachusetts, Hull was relieved that all his men had arrived back on board, safe and sound from shore leave — in fact, he had one man too many. With his sailors paraded on deck before him, Hull was about to demand a recount when the extra man, dripping wet from head to tow, stepped forward. He was a skinny fellow, stoop-shouldered and shivering. Between sobs, he announced to all present that he was Michael McGovern from the British warship POICTIERS, and that he had swum through the frigid waters from one ship to the other, "to gain freedom from the cruel Brits." He then lifted his shirt and turned his back to Hull to show him the many deep cuts on his back, hashed into his skin by a British whip. Hull, noticeably upset by the sight of the seaman's bloody and bruised back, announced that he was sorry for his ill treatment by the British, but that if he harbored a British tar aboard his ship, he would be as guilty as they in their horrid habit of impressing American seamen: McGovern would have to be returned to the

POICTIERS. McGovern fell to the deck weeping and whimpering. He begged the commander to keep him aboard and he swore that he wasn't British, but was American from Boston. McGovern spoke with a thick Irish brogue, and Hull asked him "if Dublin and not Boston might be closer to the truth."

"I meself was impressed from the American brig SUSAN BUTLER," insisted McGovern, "some eight months ago, and if you take me back to Boston, dear sir, where me sweet mither awaits me, I can prove that I am American." The American sailors were now tittering in the ranks and even Hull was forcing back a smile at the cuteness of this wiry little man. Hull was not convinced that McGovern was an American, but realized that even if it meant war, he could not return the soaked and sobbing creature that kneeled before him back to the British. "Give this man food and dry clothes," Hull's order boomed across the deck, "and then hide him below . . . Prepare to sail," he shouted to Lieutenant Morris over the cheers of his men.

Within twenty minutes of McGovern's arrival aboard the CONSTITUTION, a cutter from the POICTIERS was along side the American frigate. Aboard the cutter were ten armed British marines and Lieutenant Colson of the Royal Navy, who insisted he be allowed to come aboard to retrieve his deserter. Lieutenant Morris refused to allow him and his men aboard. "I demand to see your commander," Colson shouted up to Morris. "He's resting and can't be disturbed," replied Morris. "You'll pay for this damned Yankee insolence," cried Colson, and he ordered the cutter back to the POICTIERS.

Within a few minutes the POICTIERS was alive with activity. Her guns were being readied for action and small arms were being doled out to the crew on deck. Her battle ensign was raised to the topmast, signaling the British shore batteries and other ships in the harbor that a battle was about to commence. Hull didn't have to wait to be alerted by Lieutenant Morris. He could hear the drum rolls from the army camp, calling the Redcoats to arms. He called for all hands on deck and to battle stations.

The POICTIERS lifted her anchors to drift closer to the CONSTITUTION, then dropped them again, hardly sixty feet from her starboard side. The British and American sailors hovering over their cannons were now face to face and they began cursing and cat-calling each other. The RAZEE meanwhile, purposely drifted closer off Old Ironsides bow and dropped anchor, cutting off her escape route. Longboats filled with Redcoats were leaving the docks, obviously coming to search the CONSTITUTION to find McGovern, who was now cowering in the bilge.

Hull was bound, more than ever now, not to give up McGovern, but he was hemmed in with only 44 cannons, no match for the hundreds of loaded guns trained on him. All present realized that the spark of that inevitable war was about to ignite.

In a remarkable display of seamanship, and one which completely surprised the British, Hull made the only move left open to him without waging war — he called for his men to lift anchor and set the main topsail at an angle to the wind so that the CONSTITUTION could back out of her trap and sail in reverse towards the harbor mouth. Even though four British warships had lifted their anchors and set sail to follow him. Hull's brilliant maneuver would have been completely successful, had the wind not died before he was able to cruise out of the harbor. He was forced to drop anchor again but closer to the open sea; however, because of the lack of wind, the pursuing British vessels were forced to drop anchors as well.

Darkness set in. Hull kept his men at their stations, with an added watch around the deck, alert to possible British boarding parties. They did hear muffled oars skimming the water around them, but the Redcoats didn't attempt to board; not one shot was fired. Hull dreaded the coming of dawn, and he prayed for a breeze. It came just before dawn. The Americans had been watching throughout the night, ready to quickly hoist the sails when it came. Four British warships had been towed close to Old Ironsides in the night and were prepared for morning action, but they weren't as ready as Old Ironsides with their sails. The CONSTITUTION literally flew out of Plymouth Harbor with the new wind and headed straight out across the Atlantic. Two of the British ships tried to follow, but they were no match for Old Ironsides' speed.

McGovern, shivering from cold and fright, was escorted up from his hiding place in the bilge and allowed to become part of the crew, but it was soon discovered that he was a terrible sailor. He worked slowly and haphazardly and was afraid to climb the rigging to unfurl or set sails, because of, "a terrible fear I have of high places." The crew, who had been ready to give up their lives for him, were now angry at his laziness and fearfulness. They began taking out their frustrations on him. He was put to work in the galley, but the cook couldn't stand him — he would often have to cuff him on the side of the head to get him to do anything. Other members of the crew, when the officers weren't looking, would also give McGovern a punch, kick, or cuff, until he walked around the ship constantly flinching and ducking. When officers asked him questions, he was so frightened that he stuttered uncontrollably unable to get a word out of his mouth. Before reaching home port, Commander Hull asked Lieutenant Morris, "How's the sailor who almost started a war making out?" "He isn't worth the powder to blow him to hell," was the Lieutenant's answer. Therefore, when McGovern jumped ship in Chalrestown, nobody missed him and nobody much cared.

Considered one of the best sailors aboard the U.S.S. CONSTITUTION was Jack Lange of New Jersey, hard working, tough and fearless — a career Navy man. On June 8th, 1812, his hitch aboard Old Ironsides completed, he was transferred to the American sloop-of-war WASP which was then anchored in Boston Harbor. Jack, like Michael McGovern, had also been impressed aboard a British war ship. Unlike McGovern, the experience only made him tougher and instilled in him a desperate desire to battle the British. Jack, who had witnessed McGovern's shameful behavior aboard the CONSTITUTION, was shocked when, upon boarding the WASP, he saw the same timid stoop-shouldered character employed as a galley slave aboard the sloop. Lange hadn't seen McGovern in over a year, but there was no doubt that it was he, now thirty years of age, but looking like an old man. His hair was long and unkempt with strands of grey, deep purple bags drooped under his eyes and his thick lips were constantly quivering. Even though he stuttered every time he spoke, McGovern couldn't hide that brogue. McGovern was as fearful as ever, and Lange noticed that the crew of the WASP didn't treat him any better than had the Old Ironsides crew. He was the ship's goat, called by many unflattering names such as: "Jonah", "curr", "coward", and "dog", but McGovern seemed to take the name calling in stride. When Lange approached him and identified himself as a previous crewmember aboard the CONSTITUTION, McGovern became exceedingly nervous, his eyes darting about and his mouth twitching uncontrollably. At first he denied being the McGovern who had jumped ship at Charlestown, but then admitted to Lange that he was the one. Lange asked him why he had left one naval ship to join another, but McGovern was evasive and walked away. Next day McGovern jumped ship again.

On October 13th, as the WASP was about to weigh anchor on Atlantic war patrol, a rowboat with a woman huddled in the stern and a man straining at the oars approached the sloop. Upon reaching the anchor cable, the man jumped out of the rowboat and shimmied up the cable. As the old woman took the oars and started rowing back to

Boston, the man hauled himself aboard the WASP and landed exhausted on deck. Then he looked over the rail and waved to the old woman. "Bye bye Mither," he shouted as everyone on board roared with laughter — it was McGovern, back for more punishment. "The man is mad," Lange concluded, and from that day on, he addressed the cook's helper as "Mad Dog McGovern".

For three days after leaving port, the WASP was buffeted by gale force winds. During that time she lost her jib boom and two seamen, who were washed overboard, never to be seen again. Lange began to wonder if the WASP's last minute arrival might be a "Jonah", as seaman Bill Roberts and others had nicknamed McGovern. On the evening of October 17th however, Commander Jacob Jones spotted what he and the other WASP men, except McGovern, were looking for: six British merchant ships in convoy with a sloop-of-war, the H.M.S. FROLIC. They were heading for Halifax, Nova Scotia. The WASP followed them. At 11 a.m. the next morning, Jones brought the WASP alongside the FROLIC and hailed her Commander Whinyates. Whinyates quickly opened fire on the WASP. Jones returned the fire. The six merchant ships fled, sailing off in different directions. When the sulphur smoke cleared, Jones could see that his cannons had swept the enemy's deck, but the British cannons had cracked the WASP's topmast, ripping the headsails and killing two men who were in the rigging. A third WASP seaman, Bill Roberts, was badly wounded and was hanging precariously from the rigging high overhead. Marines in the rigging of the FROLIC were taking pot shots at him with their muskets.

The WASP was but sixty feet from the FROLIC and both crews hurriedly reloaded their cannons. Deep ocean swells almost caused the two sloops to lock bumpers. Jones could not afford any of his 110 officers and men to leave their duty stations at that moment to help Roberts, but before the second firing of the cannons, Jones noted that a man, with British musket fire whistling around him, was climbing up into the rigging. Lange quickly looked up from his twelve pounder cannon — he couldn't believe his eyes. It was McGovern in the rigging. Using a halyard, McGovern tied it around Roberts chest and was lowering him slowly to the deck.

"Fire!" shouted Jones, and the WASP's 18 cannons thundered. Almost simultaneously, the FROLIC's 22 cannons roared. The FROLIC's masts fell, covering the deck, and the WASP's mizzentop mast was shot away — most of her sails fell to the deck, as did McGovern, wrapped up in canvas like a corpse. He wriggled himself out of the sails, completely unscathed by the fall, and he carried the wounded Roberts below. One man had fallen, mortally wounded at Lange's cannon. To Lange's surprise, McGovern rushed up on deck to take the man's place. McGovern further surprised Lange by knowing exactly what to do in loading and priming a cannon. The battle between the two sloops had become a heated firing contest at close quarters, which lasted for thirty minutes. Jones ordered his cannons to fire as the WASP rolled down the crest of a swell, hoping to have the balls strike the deck or below deck where they might sink the enemy ship. Commander Whinyates, on the other hand, fired as the FROLIC nosed up over a swell, tearing the WASP's masts and rigging to pieces, with splinters showering down on the crew.

The muzzles of WASP's cannons were skimming the water — Jones brought his sloop in to ram the FROLIC. Upon doing so, Lange's cannon went right through the FROLIC's bowport. Waving a cutlass, he jumped on top of his cannon and sprang aboard the FROLIC landing on her bowsprit. McGovern, a cutlass in one hand and a pistol in the other, followed Lange. Lieutenant Biddle of the WASP attempted to join them aboard the enemy ship, but his feet got tangled in the fallen rigging causing him to fall back onto the WASP's deck. The two sloops then parted on a heavy swell, leaving Lange and McGovern alone on the FROLIC deck to battle the British in hand-to-hand combat.

Lange and McGovern found the FROLIC splattered and slippery with blood. Twenty Royal Marines with bayonets greeted them as they ran for the quarter-deck. McGovern shot one marine, then stabbed another. He sprang for the quarter-deck like an agile cat; there, Captain Whinyates, two other British officers with swords drawn, and the helmsman were waiting for him. McGovern dodged the thrust of one sword, stabbed the second officer, then quickly brought his cutlass to the captain's chin, ordering him, without the slightest trace of a stutter, to surrender his ship or be killed. The Captain immediately ordered a cease fire. Jack Lange had also disposed of two marines and was using the third as a shield to ward off the others, threatening to slash his captive's throat if the marines advanced any closer toward him or McGovern.

Commander Jones managed to bring the WASP in again to catch the FROLIC's bow, and Lieutenant Biddle successfully jumped from one ship to another. The only reason that the British hadn't struck their flag, signaling defeat to the WASP, is that none of the marines or tars dared to climb into the rigging, for fear they'd be shot. Lieutenant Biddle climbed into the rigging for them, and hauled down the British ensign. McGovern and Lange were on the quarter-deck with the British commander, two officers and the helmsmen kneeling at their feet. When Commander Jones boarded his prize, he described the FROLIC as "littered with bodies". Of the FROLIC's 135 officers, seamen and marines, 30 were dead and 50 were wounded. Aboard the WASP, five were dead and five were wounded. Lange had two bayonet wounds in his arm, but McGovern didn't have a scratch on him. The WASP crewmen were not surprised at Lange's heroics, for he had proven his valor in previous fights, but they were all amazed at McGovern's fighting spirit. They lifted the embarrassed little man to their shoulders and gave him three "Hurrahs". "He fought like a mad dog", Lange reported to his crewmates.

With both sloops badly damaged, Commander Jones decided to repair them as best he could and sail them into the closest American port. While repairs were underway, only minutes after the battle, another sail was sighted on the horizon. She was a British man-of-war, and Jones could not escape or fight her. As she closed in, one of her 78 cannons sent a warning shot across the WASP's bow. Jones had no choice, he would have to surrender his ship and his prize FROLIC. As the man-of-war came along side the WASP, Jones struck his flag.

A surging flood of fear enveloped McGovern — The British man-of-war was the H.M.S. POICTIERS, the ship he had deserted in Plymouth Harbor. Mad Dog McGovern didn't think twice about his course of action — the American and British crews watched him jump overboard, never to be seen again.

Frigate WASP, with Mad Dog McGovern aboard, battles the frigate FROLIC. Watercolor by George C. Wales, courtesy of the Peabody Museum, Salem, MA.

V
THE PROVINCETOWN PHANTOM

Salt air, sand dunes, quaint shops, and queer people, that seems to be what attracts tourists to the tiny town of Provincetown at the tip of Cape Cod — but only during the summer months. When chilling winds stir the surrounding sea, sending stinging spits of sand into the narrow streets, keepers close their shops, artists fold up their easels, and the odd couples return to their winter quarters in Boston and New York. Local fishermen then sigh contentedly, for that is when they and their families have the town to themselves — some eight months of peace and quiet after the hustle and bustle of the Summer. In 1938, however, and for many autumns and Winters thereafter, that solitude was disturbed. It was "a giant monster," said some, "a swift-footed fiend," said others, "a phantom," said Police Chief Rogers. Police Sergeant Frank Marshall called it, "the Black Flash" and the name stuck, but whatever it was, or whomever he was, the Provincetown Phantom made the cold months almost as hectic, strange, and exciting as the summer months.

He popped out of the sand dunes one October evening, an elusive superman, a super-human leaping lizard, dressed in black — all in black; black hood, black cape, black face, but his fierce eyes and long pointed ears were a glowing silver, so said the few Townies who got a glimpse of him. He was only a rumor at first, described to parents by frightened children who had seen him here and there on the dunes near the outskirts of town. Some mothers thought the creature was but a figment of their childrens' wild imaginations, whereas others thought he might be some demented fairy living in the dunes, left over from the Summer. The old fishermen laughed at the childrens' stories and called him "the bogeyman," for after all, his first appearance was just before Halloween.

It was the second week in November, however, when he first came bounding right into downtown Provincetown, frightening people off the main streets. Maria Costa was the first to be confronted by him, on Commercial Street near the Town Hall. It was dusk, and she was about to cross the street to the coffee shop, when out of the corner of her eye, she spotted someone or something lurking in the shadows of Mary Rider's boarded up art shop. The Phantom jumped out at her, "quick like a rabbit," Maria later reported to the police, "and spread his arms, like a flying bat." Maria froze in panic. She tried to scream, but no sound came out of her mouth. He hoovered over her, so close, that if she dared, she could have reached out and touched him. "He was black, all black, with eyes like balls of flame, and he was big, real big," said Maria, "maybe eight feet tall." He made a sound, a loud buzzing sound, like a Junebug on a hot day, only louder. "Then he disappeared like a flash," said Maria, leaving her in the middle of the street with her mouth wide open and her knees knocking. She ran into the coffee shop in hysterics and told the three people who were in there what had happened. Two men rushed out onto the street, but saw nothing or no one — Commercial Street was deserted. Maria was then escorted to the police station. The police thought it was funny.

Within the next three weeks, four other people had similar experiences in downtown Provincetown. The Black Flash either jumped out at them from behind a tree, or dropped down before them from a rooftop. Two of his victims were husky men, and although one man reported that he chased him, he said he was no match for the speed and agility of The Black Flash. All descriptions of the phantom seemed to match, although one of the men who was confronted by him said that he was over six feet tall, but certainly not eight feet tall. The police were now interested, but not alarmed, for their phantom had not yet hurt anyone, nor had he commited any crime.

The following Autumn the phantom returned, and his exploits were seemingly bolder this year. He continued to jump out from behind trees and leap to the sidewalk from rooftops, apparently reveling in the shocked expressions of his victims, but now, so reported five fearful and shaken witnesses, he was blowing fire from his mouth. One teenaged boy who was heading home from the library about supper time, met The Black Flash face-to-face. "It jumped out at me from nowhere," the boy told police, "and spit blue flames into my face." The boy was crying, but his face showed no signs of scorching. Farmer Charlie Farley reported that, hearing his dog barking at something under his grape vine, he grabbed his shotgun and went out into the yard to investigate. "The dog had it cornered, a giant of a thing, all in black, with long silver ears," said Farley. "I thought it was some kind of wild animal, so I shot it, and when I did, the damned thing just laughed and jumped over my eight-foot high back fence in one leap." The police now had a few suspects; a young fellow named Ford, who was a high-hurdler on an amateur track team, a local teenager named "Stretch," who was 6' 7" tall, and one of the Costa boys, who were all known around town for their practical jokes. Most of the Townies thought it might be a young fellow named Rego, who was refused a job on the police force because during the off-season months there wasn't enough activity around town to warrant another policeman. Many thought Rego had decided to make the off-season more active by becoming The Black Flash, thereby acquiring a job to help protect the town. Rego, however, was only 5' 8" tall. Whoever The Black Flash was, the police concluded, he had to be very tall, atheletic, agile, and one of the fastest runners in Provincetown. Throughout the next four years, from October to March of each year, The Black Flash continued to be active. World War II had started, and all the above named suspects had gone off to war, so the police decided it might be an out-of-towner, or possibly a very tall and strong woman.

Eightball Charlie, Provincetown's noted pool shark of the 1940's, commented one day at the poolhall, that he was convinced that The Black Flash was, "a queer in drag, who gets his kicks from scaring little kids, broads, and other fairies." His pool partner, Manuel Janard, disagreed, and related that just two evenings previous, fisherman George Loboas, a noted strongman, had been confronted by The Black Flash on the town common. "The Flash grabbed George's hand and squeezed," said Janard, "so tight that he brought George to his knees, laughing all the time he did it. George says that his laugh was like thunder, and that it was some ten minutes after The Flash had vanished that the circulation came back to his hand." "Bull!" was Charlie's reaction. "That's like the Harrington kid during the blackout the other night," he told Janard. "He said that The Black Flash grabbed his shoulder from behind, and that when he ran home, scared out of his wits, there were ice chips still on his shoulder and his arm was frozen numb for a day — Comeon Manny, you can't believe all that crap!" Manny Janard laughed. "Well, with that kind of strength, he surely ain't no fairy, he's certainly having a good time. Hell, he's driving the police nuts and he's keeping everybody home at nights."

"Well," huffed Eightball Charlie, "he ain't keeping me at home, and I'd like nothin' more than to meet that weirdo some night." Charlie's wish came true four nights later.

Charlie was walking home to the West End of town after a night of pool. It was about 9:30 and there was no moon. It was pitch black, and a chilling ocean breeze whipped up the dead leaves in the street. The trees were rocking and creaking and the low bushes lining the street along the way were constantly rustling, giving Charlie the jitters. He walked along briskly, his hands stuffed into his coat pockets. At the top of a windy hill, about a half mile from his home, a dark figure stepped out of the bushes, directly into his path. Charlie stopped in his tracks — he couldn't believe his eyes. Charlie was twenty years old and ruggedly built, but he had to admit that he was startled at seeing this massive black figure standing no more than ten feet in front of him. "Startled, but not panic stricken," he said later. With his arms streched out, each black hand holding the ends of a black cape, " he looked like a giant bat ... Yah, like Batman," said Charlie, "but staring out from under a hood were two silver eyes that glowed in the dark." The eyes glared menacingly down at Charlie. "He was a big tall man," said Charlie, " but he was a man alright, not a monster or anything like that." They looked at each other, unmoving, for what seemed like five minutes to Charlie — and then Charlie yelled, sort of a half angry, half frightened yell, "hoping to scare him off," said Charlie. "Then I shouted at him, 'You'd better get out of my way, or I'll smack you one !' "

The Black Flash then moved, but not out of the way — he stepped towards Charlie, brought up his left hand, and slapped Charlie so hard across the face that he fell backwards. The next thing Charlie remembered was that he was running as fast as he could towards home, with The Black Flash close on his heels. He made the front door, huffing and puffing, then slammed and locked it behind him. Charlie was known around town, not only as a pool-shark, but as a good sprinter, but as he told Manny Janard the next morning, "The Black Flash was right behind me all the way."

"So you were scared," said Manny.

Charlie blushed, "Yah, I guess I was, but only after he slapped me so hard." A red mark from the hand of The Black Flash was still noticeable on Charlie's right cheek the next day. The police now had a new clue, The Black Flash was probably left handed.

There were only some 4,500 permanent residents in Provincetown, and these frightened people kept pressuring the police to either capture The Black Flash, or at least come up with some clues as to whom he might be. For one entire year, the police were convinced that the phantom was a local teenager named John Williams. He was tall, quick on his feet, and his hobby was lifting weights — even his pals called him "Flash" Williams, but on the night Eightball Charlie was attacked, John Flash Williams was in Tiverton, Rhode Island, a seaman aboard a freighter.

The children of Provincetown were, of course, frightened out of their wits, and their parents had no trouble getting them into the house once the sun went down — many even refused to go out trick-or-treating on Halloween Night.

It was a cold November afternoon in 1945, when Allen Janard, Manuel Janard's 13 year old cousin, went trudging up Standish Street with a stack of funnybooks tucked under his arm. He was on his way to Manny's house, some six blocks away, to trade funnybooks. Both were avid collectors of Superman, Batman, and Captain-Marvel comics. Manny, then 18 years old, browsed through Al's funnybooks, as Al flipped though the pages of his. The trade was made, and Al anxious to get back home to read his thrity or more new comics, thanked his cousin and was about to start out the front door when he noticed it was already dark outside. Manny saw the twinge of fear on Allen's face, but did not offer to walk him home. After all, Allen lived only a few blocks away, almost in the middle of downtown Provincetown. Allen tucked the load of funnybooks under his arm, and Manny watched him trot down the street. Then Allen started running, as fast as he could. No one else was on the streets and he was scared. Up one hill and down, finding relief in his troubled mind only when his house came into view at the foot of the hill. He squeeked open the white gate leading to the front walk, but didn't see the massive shadow hiding behind the rose-bushes. It leaped out at him, and the funnybooks went flying into the air. It wasn't one of his older brothers playing a trick on him, it was The Black Flash, here, standing before him in his own front yard, no more than twenty yards from his front door. Allen screamed, a blood-curdling scream, and his legs almost folded under him. This phantom that he had heard so many stories about, was enormous, much bigger than he had imagined. Its face was so evil looking that Allen had to turn his own face away, and its horrid laugh, more like a deep gurgle, penetrated his eardrums.

"Joey, Louie," Allen screamed at the top of his lungs, knowing that his older brothers must be in the house. The front light over the door went on — someone had heard his screams. Allen tried to dodge around The Black Flash, but the creature jumped in front of him again, blocking his way. Allen fell to his knees, hysterical. Then, quickly and seemingly with little effort, the phantom leaped over the front gate and disappeared down the street. It took almost twenty minutes for Allen to recover and calm down enough to tell his mother and brothers what had happened. Not one of the Janards ventured out of the house again that evening, but in the morning Allen went out to collect his funnybooks — they were scattered everywhere, all over the front lawn and street.

That same evening, only two hours after young Allen Janard's encounter, Sergeant Francis Marshall of the Provincetown police force got a call from an elderly woman living near the Governor-Bradford School. She had seen The Black Flash sneaking into the school yard. No sooner had Sergeant Marshall hung up, when another caller reported similar information — The Black Flash was in the Bradford Schoolyard

— and the yard was surrounded by a ten-foot fence, with only one way in or out. Maybe, thought Marshall, this was his chance to capture Provincetown's elusive pest. The police had been getting calls and tips on The Black Flash for years. Sometimes he seemed to be two places at once, or, he'd be reported on one side of town, and a moment later, someone would call and say he was on the other side of town, two miles away.

Two patrol cars converged at the school yard entrance, without lights and without sirens blaring. One policeman went around the outside of the fence and three, including Marshall, walked around the school building to the backyard carrying flashlights. Within minutes, one of the policemen shouted, "I've got him!" They all rushed in. There, facing them in the beam of a flashlight, cornered by the fence on three sides and the policemen in front of him, was The Black Flash. In the beam of light, Marshall could see that the evil face was a mask, which looked like an old flour-screen without its handle, painted silver and strapped to the phantom's head. He was tall, concluded Marshall, but not as tall as most of his victims had described him, but he certainly was bold, for as the police approached, warning him not to move, he laughed at them, a deep, husky laugh, which echoed through the flour-screen mask. Hands on hips, he turned his head from side to side, watching as the four policemen advanced on him. Then, he bolted for the fence, and in one great leap, he had grabbed the top of it, and was over. The police didn't have a chance, and as Marshall reported, "he disappeared in a flash."

A few weeks later, on a cold December afternoon, with a thick fog rolling in from the sea, Allen Janard, his younger sister, Elanore, and his two brothers, were playing hide-and-seek in their back yard on Standish Street. On the sandy hill overlooking the yard, Elanore spotted something crouching. "Look," she shouted, "there's a bear on the hill." The boy laughed. "There's no bears on Cape Cod," Allen informed her. "I've never seen a bear," Elanore admitted, "but if that isn't a bear, what is it?" The boys looked up and saw something crawling down the hill towards them, barely visible in the fog. Allen recognized it immediately, and a numbing fear flooded his body. He gave the alarm and they all ran for the house to cower in the kitchen. Their parents weren't home and the kitchen door lock was broken. Out the window, they watched the black figure run into the back yard and head for the back door. Joey grabbed his mother's rolling pin, Allen held a carving knife over his head, and Louie quickly filled a bucket with scalding water. Elanore hid behind a chair. All the crying and screaming in the kitchen suddenly died to an eerie silence as the backdoor doorknob began to turn. "All I could hear was my heartbeat," said Allen, but the door didn't open. The fearless phantom just remained outside the backdoor, breathing heavily, so they'd know he was still there. Louie then got an idea, he went up through the house with his bucket of water to the attic and, through the skylight, got out onto the roof. Crawling down the overhang over the kitchen, he spied the black figure below and dumped his bucket. Inside the kitchen, the others heard the splash and a grunt, which Elanore insisted was the growl of a bear. Then through the window, they saw him retreat through the back yard, a dripping black phantom, shivering from head to toe, not looking half as fearsome as he had when he arrived — and that was the last anyone in Provincetown saw of The Black Flash.

Who was he? In looking back, Allen Janard, now in his mid-fifties, thinks it might have been his cousin, Manny Janard; Matt Costa, now a prominent businessman in Provincetown, always thought it was his brother Elmer, but both those suspects were only 12 and 13 years old when the Provincetown Phantom made his first appearance. Francis Marshall, who became Provincetown's Police Chief in 1959, and is now retired, living in Yarmouth, told me that he knows who The Black Flash was, "but I won't give you a name," the former police chief told me. "I will tell you this though," he said, "The Black Flash wasn't just one person. He was four men, who sometimes played the part alone, and sometimes together. Two are dead now, but the others have a hell of a time when they get together, reminiscing about the times they scared the hell out of their friends and neighbors in Provincetown." The Provincetown Phantom, better known as The Black Flash, is legend now, and his daring exploits, agility, strength and size grow greater and greater as the years go by.

Al Janard relates his encounter with the Provincetown Phantom.

VI
SPRINGFIELD'S SEEDY SAINT

He was short and wiry, quiet and unkempt. "A strange lad," his Uncle Ben Mann had called him, "A queer boy," a neighboring farmer had said. Yet, monuments have been erected to him from Mansfield, Ohio to Springfield, Massachusetts, and some say he never lived at all — that he was an imaginary person, a myth, merely a legend.

He was born and baptized Jonathan Chapman, in Leominster, Massachusetts on September 24, 1774, six months and 24 days before the Battle of Lexington and Concord. On that memorable day in American history, his father, Nat Chapman, grabbed his musket from its place over the kitchen mantle, and went off to join George Washington's little rag-tag army. Nat remained with Washington through Valley Forge, but less than a year after he had left home, his wife died. Baby Jonathan and his two older sisters were sent to nearby Lunenburg, Massachusetts, to live with their uncle and aunt, Mr. and Mrs. David Chapman. Nat returned home from Valley Forge with frost-bitten feet, yet he remained in the Colonial Army and was stationed at the armory in Springfield, Massachusetts. It was at nearby Longmeadow, then a part of Springfield, that he met Lucie Cooley, a farmer's daughter; they were soon married. Once setttled into the Cooley farm at Longmeadow, Nat sent for his three children to come live with him and Lucie. Jonathan, then age eight, was not anxious to leave his loving aunt and uncle, and although Lucie was a loving stepmother, she had little time for him, for she soon produced ten more children for Nat Chapman, five girls and five boys.

Jonathan, being the oldest boy, was forced to work long hours about the farm, helping support the large Chapman family. He was also constantly hired out by his father to help neighboring farmers. The Chapman home, with so many squaking infants, was a constantly loud and hectic place, and Jonathan, an introverted boy who prefered peace and quiet, felt more at home in the barn with the farm animals. He did, however, enjoy planting and harvesting crops, and was noted around the Springfield area by farmers as having a "green thumb". Although there was no time for formal schooling at Springfield, Jonathan had learned to read and write while living at Lunenburg. One history lesson about America's first white settlers, left a strong impression: When John Endicott, first Governor of Massachusetts Bay Company, came to Salem in 1628 to establish America's first commercial outpost, he immediately wrote back to the authorities in England requesting that peach, cherry, pear, plum, and apple plants be shipped to him in quantity on the next boat. The fruit scions arrived at Salem in the early summer of 1630 and Endicott planted them on 300 acres of land at Salem Village, and here, but for berries and wild grapes, were America's first fruits. On every New England farm which Jonathan had ever visited or worked, these fruit trees were growing, all the offspring of Endicott's orchard. He had read and heard many fascinating stories about Governor Endicott, and considered him the most courageous and far-sighted of American leaders.

Besides history and husbandry, Jonathan enjoyed hiking- a healthy, seemingly harmless pursuit, but when he became a teenager, his father began worrying about his wander-lust. Many times when needed on the farm, Jon would go off on long hikes, often traveling 50 to 100 miles, and he'd be gone for days. He'd walk to Lunenburg to see his aunt and uncle, or up to Worcester, or down to Hartford, Connecticut. One of his favorite destinations was Mason, New Hampshire, some sixty miles from Springfield. Here, his uncle Benjamin Mann lived in a square white house on the village green. Benjamin had been a hero in the Battle of Bunker Hill, and now owned the store and tavern at Mason, which was part of the house. He was a fat, jolly, outspoken man, who wasn't especially fond of his quiet, withdrawn nephew. Therefore, it must be concluded that Jonathan didn't walk all the way to Mason to see Uncle Ben. The store and tavern were managed by a happy-go-lucky freed black slave named Christopher, who was constantly quoting the Bible, and who made delicious Johnny Cakes whenever Jon arrived. Possibly, he was the reason Jonathan traveled so far from home. However, Uncle Ben also had a pretty daughter named Betsey, who was Jonathan's own age, and she certainly was a factor in enticing him away from the farm.

Kind hearted Betsey Mann liked her first cousin, even though he was a bit shy, and didn't seem to care much about the patched clothes he wore when he came visiting. She found him interesting, especially when he talked about the things he had seen in his travels, and the wonders of the Wild West that he had heard about from others. Many New Englanders were picking up bag and baggage, selling their homes and land for conastoga wagons, and heading West for greener pastures. Young Jonathan was determined that some day he'd join them.

There were only a few other teenagers living in the sleepy village of Mason, and Betsey truly enjoyed Jonathan's company, but Jonathan had a loud thumping in his heart, which he knew wasn't from all the hard walking. Betsey's best friends were the Wilson girls who lived on a neighboring farm. It wasn't long before Jonathan found that Betsey was sweet on their older brother, Sam Wilson. Outwardly, Jonathan seemed to take it in stride, for he liked Sam Wilson too, and they often talked about heading West together. Jonathan felt his second twinge of jealousy the day Sam turned 20 and announced to Betsey and him, that he and his brother Eben Wilson were striking out to the new frontier — they were trekking off to the wilderness of Upstate New York. Betsey was broken hearted, even though Sam said that he's someday return for her, and Jon shuffled his way back to Springfield, knowing that, one way or another, he would soon head for the wild frontier too — and maybe Betsey would cry when he said goodbye.

There were many strange and fascinating stories that came out of the West and filtered East in the early 19th Century — many exaggerated tales of Indian attacks, cowboy shoot-outs and lost gold mines, but there was one story, retold many times, about an eccentric man wearing long whiskers and funny clothes, who did nothing but walk around in the wilderness planting seeds. "He has to be crazier than a hoot-owl," most Easterners concluded — they called him "Johnny Appleseed" — his real name was Jonathan Chapman.

He came out of Pennsylvania and into the Ohio Territory in about 1801, so the story went. He was, at first, on horseback, with four leather sacks filled with pear and apple seeds strapped to the saddle. His first stop was at Isaac Stadden's farm in Licking County, and there, along the shores of Licking Creek, he planted his seeds, which became Ohio's first orchard. He then proceeded from one farm to the next; and five years later, two trappers reported seeing him in a canoe filled with apple seeds in Jefferson County, Ohio, paddling into Indiana Territory — America's most Western frontier. A few year later, he was spotted back in Western Pennsylvania at a cider mill, collecting more seeds to plant. He got the seeds free, for when the ripe apples were pressed in the mill, the seeds were usually thrown away.

With heavy bags of seeds thrown over his shoulder, he headed West again, this time by foot. The only other item he carried was the Holy Bible. When his shoes wore out, he went barefooted, even through the snow, when his buckskins wore out, he wore a burlap coffee sack with holes cut in to it for his arms and head. In Detroit, Michigan, he was seen leaving an Indian village in the dead of winter, with a boot on one foot and an Indian moccasin on the other. At Fort Duquesne, frontiersmen reported that he wore a "triangular pasteboard hat," to protect his eyes from the glare of the sun. At Fort Sandusky, he wore a coon-skin cap, and at the Black Fork of the Mohican, an Indian reported that he wore "a tin mush-pot for a hat".

Jonathan Chapman didn't just plant seeds throughout America's West, he planted Bible scripture in the minds and hearts of anyone who would listen, including the Indians. Visiting American wilderness forts, farms, or Indian villages, the children swarmed him, for he always brought gifts of wooden figures which he had whittled, and he'd tell funny stories that he had made up as he went along. He also talked to the children about the importance of being kind to animals and even insects. The Indians considered him a great Medicine Man, for besides apple and pear seeds, he would scatter seeds of herbs used for healing, such as catnip, hoarhound, pennyroyal, and dog-fennel, which he felt helped to cure malaria. At one Indian battle near Mansfield, Ohio, Jonathan nursed the wounded on both sides of the fight with his herb medicines, and then lectured his Indian friends that fighting was wrong.

Jon befriended many people as he walked from place to place, and many animals as well. One of his travel companions, for many years, was a wolf that he found abandoned and dying in the woods as a pup. Indians of Michigan reported that, after being bitten by a rattle-snake, he petted the snake and soothed it of its fright, before he squeezed its poison from his hand. "Johnny Appleseed" became bigger than life. The story of his real life became so mixed with legend, that even today, many people don't believe that he ever existed — but he was here, in fact, he was just about everywhere.

On a hot Spring evening in 1847, a little old man with white whiskers, wearing a burlap shirt, baggy pants tied to his waist with a rope, no hat and no shoes walked up the long dirt drive to the home of William Worth in Allen County, Indiana. The old man carried what seemed to be an empty leather sack over his shoulder. He knocked lightly at the farmhouse door and Mrs, Worth answered.

"For some chore about the farm," he asked, "could I bother you for a slice of bread and a drink of water?"

The old man looked tired, yet Mrs. Worth noted a lively sparkle in his eyes, and smiling cracks about his lips. "Certainly, you may have your fill without performing a chore," said Mrs. Worth, and she went to the kitchen to fetch a large slice of bread with butter and a cup of milk. She delivered it to the old man, who sat on the stoop to eat and drink.

"May God bless you for this kindness," he said. "I've walked twenty miles this day, and this food is most refreshing."

William Worth walked to the house from the fields, his work for the day complete, and introduced himself to the old man.

"I am Jonathan Chapman," said the old man, "wandering this great country of ours, planting God's food in the earth and God's words in the minds of men, so that Uncle Sam may reap."

"How far have you wandered thus far?" asked Farmer Worth.

"Over one hundred square miles," he replied, smiling up at the surprised look on Worth's face, "but it's taken me over forty-seven years to do it," he explained.

"And where are you going now?" asked Mrs. Worth.

"I'm going home," he said, staring over the fields, "I'm going home."

The Worths asked Jonathan to spend the night. At first he refused, saying that he prefered sleeping in the woods, but cooling winds and the threat of a storm, prompted him to reluctantly agree to remain the night under their roof. He would not sleep in a bed though. "Too much comfort would spoil the likes of me," he told them, so he curled up on the kitchen floor. From their bedroom, the Worths heard old Jonathan mumbling Christ's Beatitudes before he fell asleep.

In the morning, Mrs. Worth was startled when she came into the kitchen. Old Jonathan was still lying on the floor, but, as she reported later, "his features were all aglow with a spernal light." Johnny Appleseed, age 73, was dead, his labors over — he had gone Home.

William Worth also saw the bright, halo-like light surrounding Jon Chapman's body. "It shone for some twenty minutes," he said, "then dissipated." The Worths could not understand what caused the light, nor did they know its meaning. Jonathan was buried not far from the Worth farm, at Archer's Graveyard near Fort Wayne. Word of his death spread quickly through the Country, and when the United States Congress heard of his passing, all members stood silently in prayer. Senator Sam Houston gave the eulogy, in which he said, "This old man was one of the most useful citizens in the world. His labor was a labor of love, and generations yet unborn will rise up and call him blessed."

Jonathan Chapman remembered his childhood pals, Betsey and Sam of Mason, New Hampshire, until his dying day. He felt there was something special, even sacred in their meeting and playing together on the Mason New Hampshire green. Certainly, the love and teachings of former slave Christopher had some effect on his life. His love for Betsey and his desire to follow Sam into the wilderness did too.

Sam Wilson, as promised, had returned to Mason and married Betsey Mann in 1797, and together they had returned to Troy, New

York. In later years, because of their love and dedication to the people, and especially the children of Upstate New York, they were fondly known as "Aunt Betsey" and "Uncle Sam." Sam owned a successful packing company in Troy, and during the war, he stamped all his barrels of beef "U.S.", meaning United States, but the soldiers in the War of 1812, were jokingly told that the initials stood for "Uncle Sam". Soon, recruiting posters with Sam Wilson's portrait on them were being displayed about New York. Thus, Sam Wilson became the Uncle Sam we know today, America's patron saint. Jonathan Chapman was also a saint, sewing seeds and scripture across the land, as he said, "so Uncle Sam may reap" — Johnny Appleseed was America's, and one of God's, most blessed saints — The fruits of his labor throughout America, are living monuments to his greatness.

America's first pear and apple trees were shipped to Salem from England by Governor Endecott in 1630, and he planted an orchard in Salem Village, now Danvers, MA. One of his pear trees is still standing and bearing fruit, although it was severely damaged in the 1938 hurricane. Endecott was Johnny Appleseed's inspiration to plant these trees in the West.

The Village Green in Mason, New Hampshire, where Johnny Appleseed, Uncle Sam and Aunt Betsey played together as children. Betsey Mann's home, once her father's store and tavern, as shown here, still stands facing the Green. Photo by Travis Smith.

VII
THE LONG AND THE SHORT OF IT

There is a New England legend that giant Indians once roamed our forests and fields. Nothing concrete is available today to substantiate the existence of oversized Indians, but all legend, it seems has a grain of truth to it, and so there may have been at one time a tribe of giants, or maybe just a few big Indians living here. They were possibly wiped out in a tribal battle, or maybe by the plague that ravaged New England only a few years before white men and women first settled at Plymouth in 1620.

Increase Mather, President of Harvard College in 1712, tried to prove their existence to the Royal Society of London by presenting a detailed formal letter about a 17 foot long thigh bone and a five pound tooth that were unearthed in New England that year. Mather stated that the thigh bone and tooth proved that a race of giants lived on earth before the great flood. The bones obviously belonged to some prehistoric beast, but Mather convinced many New Englanders that they were the remains of a giant Indian.

There were, of course, occasional giants that did crop up from time-to-time in this area, one being David Bubier, known in his native state of Maine as the "Aroostock Giant." By today's standards he wasn't too exceptional — only seven feet tall — but he weighed 360 lbs. and in the 1820's, he was considered the biggest man in America. What David was missing in brains, he made up for in brawn.

It wasn't until 1833, when he was in his prime, that New Englanders began hearing about David. That winter he, his sister Lydia and brother Charles strode into Fort Fairfield from their mountain home. Their parents had passed on and the children decided to move from their mountain cabin to the fort. They carried all their possessions with them, David carrying the bulk of the load: a bed, table, two chairs, and a stove, all strapped to his back. It wasn't just his size and the load he carried that amazed the people of Fort Fairfield, but that he had walked the many miles down the mountain, through the snow, barefooted. His feet were frostbitten when he arrived at the fort but David's feet were size 22, and there wasn't a pair of shoes in the country that would fit him.

Because of his size and strength, David was hired to carry the mail between Fort Fairfield and Houlton, Maine. Surely no highwayman or Indian would tangle with the likes of him to get at the mail. Proper foot covering was a problem for their giant mailman but the local blacksmith made a pair of clodhoppers for David out of two ox-yokes. To add to David's delight, a local Indian chief made him a pair of large snowshoes. In the winter months, David made good time from Fairfield to Houlton in his snowshoes; better time than any Indian mail carrier.

David left his mail route and he moved on to become a lumberjack. He truly enjoyed this labor and was so excited with his new ax that even on days off he would romp through the woods felling trees. "I love the sound of them falling," he said. In his spare time, he would also go hunting moose with rocks. He'd spot a moose and hurl a boulder at it, and his aim was usually on the mark. The old boys of Aroostock say that David had quite an appetite, and could consume an entire moose within a few days. There were twenty eye-witnesses at the logging camp store who saw him drink a gallon barrel of thick molasses within twenty minutes.

One day, a bear trainer entered the lumber camp and challenged any man there to wrestle his bear to the ground. Five tough French Canadian lumberjacks tried and failed and, in the process, were badly mauled by the bear. After betting and losing their hard-earned wages to the trainer, the loggers called on David to fight the bear. In the tussle that ensued, the bear cut David's leg with its sharpened claws. This angered David to put on a show of strength that the onlookers could hardly believe. He lifted the bear over his head and threw it over a steep embankment into a rocky river. Seeing his meal ticket groaning in the river bed, the trainer lashed out at David with his whip. David caught the stinging whip across his face, but managed to wrestle the weapon from the trainer. He then lifted the trainer over his head and tossed him into the river with the bear. David's leg wound never healed properly, and he soon left the logging camp never to be heard from again, but the stories of his prowess live on in Maine, and were instrumental in creating the legend of the famous lumberjack, Paul Bunyan.

The most famous giant from America's north east was not a strongman, but was world renowned for sweetness and beauty. She was Anna Swan, the Nova Scotia Giantess. Anna measured 2½ feet at birth, weighed 24 pounds, and her feet were 5½ inches long. Both her parents were over six feet tall, but at age 15, she looked down at them. She blossomed into a beautiful, well-proportioned young lady of 7½ feet.

Still in her teens, she left her parents and twelve brothers and sisters at Pictou, Nova Scotia and traveled to Boston and then to New York to appear in P.T. Barnum's American Museum, where she was billed as "the tallest woman in the world." She often appeared on stage with midget Tom Thumb, who was 25 inches tall, and with Issac Sprague the "Skeleton Man," who was 5 feet 4 inches tall, but weighed only 52 pounds. Issac, who was born in East Bridgewater, Massachusetts in 1841, began losing weight for some unknown reason when he was 12 years old. "I began to lose not only my flesh, but my muscles," explained Issac, "until I could no longer work in the Bridgewater grocery store and decided to join the circus."

Issac became extremely fond of Anna Swan and she of him. Most of the people working at the American Museum felt it was a strong friendship rather than a romance, but these same people were quick to admit that in the circus atmosphere of unique sizes and shapes, opposites did attract. It was Issac who saved Anna's life in November of 1864 when a fire destroyed the American Museum. Anna had panicked when the fire started, and Issac managed to pull and push all 400 pounds of her down a flight of stairs and out a back door that she could barely squeeze through. It was later discovered that the fire was set by Captain Robert Kennedy of the Confederate Army in retaliation for General Sherman's devastation of the South.

Less than a year later, July 13, 1865, another fire broke out in the New York boarding house where the circus performers were staying. Issac was living on the fifth floor and Anna on the third. Endangering his own life, Issac raced down the smoke filled stairways to Anna's side, but this time he couldn't budge her. She was in hysterics and frozen with fear. The New York Tribune wrote the story as follows:

"Anna's best friend, the living skeleton, stood by her as long as he dared, but then deserted her to get help. As the heat grew in intensity, the perspiration rolled from her face in rivulets . . . As a last resort, the employees of the place procured a loft derrick and erected it alongside the museum. It took eighteen men on a line to lower her from the third floor to the ground level."

Anna was rushed to the hospital with her feet sticking out the back door of the ambulance. She nearly lost her life and did lose all her savings in the fire. On March 3, 1868, the museum caught fire again and Anna, once more, barely escaped with her life and lost the money she had saved since the previous fire. After this third fire, P.T. Barnum announced his retirement, and Anna joined another circus troupe on a tour through Europe. It was on this tour that she met Captain Martin Bates, a Kentucky cavalryman who stood 7 feet 2½ inches and weighed 470 pounds. It was love at first sight for both of them. For those who could see that high, Anna and Martin made a handsome couple. They were married in London on June 17, 1871. The bride's diamond ring was a gift from Queen Victoria.

A year later, the gigantic couple had a child. She was 2 feet tall and weighed 18 pounds, but died at birth. Returning to the United States, Captain Bates built a special home for his wife in Seville, Ohio, with ceilings 14 feet high and doorways 8½ feet high. All the large furniture was handmade by the Captain himself. The couple moved in and worked a farm until 1888 when Anna died on her 42nd birthday. Nine years earlier, she had given birth to a second child. He lived only one day, but at birth, weighed 24 pounds and was 2½ feet tall. A life-sized plastic statue of the baby boy is at the Cleveland, Ohio Health Museum, displayed as, "the biggest baby ever born." Anna's husband died in 1919.

Today, a person measuring 6' 6" is not considered a giant, and seven-footers are seen on many basketball courts. The recent President of the Massachusetts Senate, Kevin Harrington of Salem, is 6' 8" tall, and has proven to be a man to look up to in more ways than one. The average height of each succeeding generation of Americans increases by one or two inches, which means , that by the year 2,263, the average American will be about 6' 6" tall.

Up until the mid-twentieth century, doctors and scientists had little knowledge as to the reasons why a person became a midget or a giant. Today, it is known that the pituitary gland at the base of the brain determines human growth. This gland produces a hormone called HGH into the system. If an excess of HGH is produced, the person becomes a giant; and if too little is produced, he or she is a midget or dwarf. Dwarfism can also be caused by thyroid conditions, diabetes and other diseases, but usually the pituitary gland is the cause. To be scientifically considered a dwarf or midget, one must be less than 4 feet 6 inches tall. Most African pygmies, therefore, do not fit into this class, for their average height is just under 5 feet. The difference between midgets and dwarfs is that midgets are perfectly formed little people; whereas, dwarfs are not perfectly proportioned and usually have some sort of deformity.

The most famous Americn dwarfs were Wano and Plutano, otherwise known as "The Wild Men of Borneo." They were neither wild men, nor were they from Borneo; they were from Weston, Massachusetts.

Hiram and Barney Davis were discovered by P.T. Barnum, who advertised that he had purchased them from a sea captain who had captured them in the jungles of Borneo. They appeared on stage wearing leopard skins, in a cage or in chains, grunting and growling at the thousands of people who came to stare at them. They were only three feet tall, weighed 50 pounds apiece, had straggly beards, and wore their hair in braids. Hiram, or Wano, as Barnum called him, could lift a 200 pound man over his head, and Plutano, who had dainty little hands, could scramble up and down his cage like a monkey. The Wild men traveled the world, putting on their act, but their real home was Waltham, Massachusetts, where they lived with their manager Hanaford Warner.

In the Warner home, all the doorknobs were lowered so that the dwarfs could freely roam the house and two high chairs were set at the kitchen table. Mrs. Warner never was able to teach Wano and Plutano table manners. "They ate like apes," she once commented. They couldn't talk, but understood each other by emitting variously pitched grunts. They were playful and acted much like three year-old children, but they obeyed commands and understood some of what was going on around them. When Mrs. Warner took them for a walk in Waltham, she would cover their heads with hoods.

Wano left the circus business after he attempted to lift a man weighing over 400 pounds over his head. Wano slipped and the man fell on him. Wano was never the same again. He died at age 80 in 1905. Plutano lived to be 85 and died in 1912.

The most popular and revered midget who ever lived was Charles Sherwood Stratton of Bridgeport, Connecticut. He was born on January 4, 1838, weighing 9 pounds, 2 ounces. At five months old he weighed 15 pounds and was two feet tall; but at five years old, he was the same weight and height. Also living in Bridgeport at the time was the 33 year old, already famous, Phineas T. Barnum, America's number one showman. Phineas, hearing about the 24 inch boy who lived in his own hometown, asked Mr. Stratton to bring his son over to visit. Young Charles was shy at first, but he soon took a liking to the 6 foot 2 inch Barnum, and the father was willing to let little Charlie appear at New York's American Museum. Recalling the old fairy tale about the little knight who rode a mouse in King Arthur's Court, Phineas decided "we'll call him Tom Thumb."

Barnum, who had no qualms about exaggerating, announced to the press that Tom Thumb was eleven years old and just arrived from England. Before his debut, however, Barnum taught Charles Stratton how to sing, dance and tell jokes. He then marched the streets of New York and into every newspaper office with Tom Thumb perched on his shoulder. "The little man was entertaining and witty and the smallest specimen of man we've ever seen," wrote the Herald — and Tom Thumb was on his way to stardom. He won the hearts of Americans, and then Barnum and Tom Thumb sailed away to Europe.

In London, Barnum had a custom made coach, drawn by two 34 inch tall Shetland ponies for Tom to ride in through the streets, and the Queen of England was thrilled by the little man's talent and intellect. Tom was showered with gifts from Europe's royalty, and he returned to America a millionaire. In 1855, when Barnum was near bankruptcy from bad investments, it was Tom Thumb who saved him by providing money for him to get his show started again.

When Tom was 24 years old, at height 34 inches and weighing 52 pounds, he fell in love. The girl of his dreams was also from New England — Lavinia Warren, who was 32 inches tall and weighed 29 pounds. She was born in Middleboro, Massachusetts in 1841. When Tom spotted her at the American Museum, he trudged into Barnum's office and said, "Sir, that is the most charming lady I have ever seen, and I believe God created her on purpose to be my wife."

Tom, however, soon found he had a rival to deal with before obtaining Lavinia's hand in marriage. His name was George Washington Morrison Nutt, better known as Commodore Nutt. Nutt was a young man of 18 from New Hampshire, who was 29 inches tall and weighed 24 pounds. Like Tom, he was talented and witty; unlike Tom, he was quick-tempered and jealous. In their first encounter with Lavinia, Nutt knocked Tom to the ground.

If Tom couldn't outfight young Nutt, he could outfox him. Hearing that Lavinia was a guest at Barnum's house at Bridgeport, Tom arrived, and Barnum, of course, welcomed him. Persuading Barnum to go to bed early, Tom proposed to Lavinia in Barnum's living room and she accepted. An hour later, who should arrive at Barnum's front door but Commodore Nutt. He marched straight up to Barnum's bedroom and accused the startled showman of interfering in a love triangle. "You're too late Nutt," shouted Tom Thumb, "Lavinia and I are to be married."

Nutt was heartbroken, but was gentleman enough to shake Tom's hand, kiss the bride-to-be on the cheek and leave the house. To make amends, Tom persuaded Nutt to be his best man, and the maid-of-honor was Minnie Warren, Lavinia's sister, who Commodore Nutt immediately took a liking to. The wedding in miniature, with over 1,000 guests attending, was held on February 10, 1863. Although the Civil War was in full swing, the wedding made front page headlines in every major American newspaper.

On the honeymoon, Mr. and Mrs. Tom Thumb visited President Abe Lincoln in Washington. The tall, lanky President commented that Lavinia bore a striking resemblance to his own wife. He also asked Tom his opinion of the war. "P.T. Barnum would settle the whole affair in a month," replied Tom. As Lincoln bent down to bid the little couple farewell, he said: "God likes to do funny things, and here we are, the long and the short of it."

For the next four years Tom, Lavinia, Commodore Nutt and Lavinia's sister Minnie toured the world. During the tour, Commodore Nutt was edged out again when Minnie decided to marry skater Edward Newell, who had been traveling with them. Newell was short, but not a midget, and he returned with Minnie to Middleboro to live. Less than a year later Minnie gave birth to a 5½ pound baby boy, but Minnie died in childbirth, as did her baby.

In 1883, tragedy befell Tom and Lavinia when the Milwaukee hotel they were staying at caught fire. The two midgets were caught in the blaze and only at the last minute were saved by a fireman who carried them to safety. The experience was too much for Tom, and he died soon after at his home in Middelboro on July 15, 1883, at age 45 — "and that was the long and short of it."

Maine claims to be the home of Paul Bunyon. His statue stands tall in Bangor. Photo by Jim Walsh.

Linc Hawkes' red barn at Redd's Pond and part of his cluttered front yard, Marblehead, MA.

VIII
THE LIVING LEGEND OF LINC HAWKES

I first met Henryetta in 1954, when I was 18 years old. I worked at Graves Yacht Yard in Marblehead, but after work one evening my chore was to deliver supper to Henryetta from Maddie's Sail Loft Restaurant, the local watering hole for yard workers and fishermen. Henryetta lived with Lincoln Hawkes on Norman Street, beside Redd's Pond, only a few hundred yards up the hill from Maddie's Sail Loft. I was delivering the bag of food as a favor to Kenny Duncan, owner of Maddie's, for it took me only a few streets out of the way to my own home at Goodwin's Landing. My parents and I had moved to Marblehead only a couple of years earlier from neighboring Salem, however, I quickly discovered that living in Marblehead was like living in another world.

Marblehead is a rocky peninsula jutting out into the Atlantic, somewhat isolated from the rest of Massachusetts. Its first resident, other than the Indians, was fisherman Joseph Dollaber, who was kicked out of Salem in 1629, because of his, "continuous thirst for rum," and who rowed across to Marblehead on a hogshead barrel. He lived in the barrel for the rest of his long life, fishing and trading with the Indians, and became the founder of Marblehead. Today, quaint Revolutionary War vintage homes hug her narrow winding streets in Town, and majestic mansions dot the high cliffs along the shore. Her population is a mix of crusty fishermen and eccentric millionaires, mostly Republican Yankees who don't like outsiders coming to live in their town, especially Irish Democrats like myself.

"You're not a Marbleheader unless your grandfather was born here," any old Townie will tell you. I once heard Linc Hawkes say, "If I ain't a Marbleheader, then there ain't no such thing as a Marblheader."

Linc Hawkes worked at Graves Yacht Yard too, as a mechanic and rigger of sailing ships, but he wasn't full time. He worked only when he felt like it, or when Mr. Graves could persuade him to come down to the yard to work on some special project or solve some ticklish problem. Linc was noted for his creativity and craftsmanship, as well as for his stern independence and surprising eccentricities. Most of his life had been spent on the high seas as a fisherman and merchant marine. He was a captain of a power-yacht at age 16. During World War II, he joined the Coast Guard, and the military leaders also became aware of his unique abilities, for they made him a Marine, without even asking his permission. On extended temporary duty as a Leather-Neck, Linc taught the Marines how to maneuver landing barges into beach-heads and, more important, how to get them off the beach again. After the war, Linc fished out of Alaska for three years, then returned to Marblehead to build his own home on the banks of Redd's Pond, beneath Old Burying Hill. He got married, but that didn't last "and now," so Kenny Duncan informed me, "he lives with Henryetta."

I arrived at 7 Norman Street with her food at about dusk, and was awe struck, for I could see no house. There was an old red barn sitting beside the pond, and an array of boats on cradles facing the street; fishing boats, sailboats, dories, power launches, and one with a "For Sale" sign on it that looked for all the world like Noah's Ark. There were also two large refrigerator trucks, smelling fishy and dripping rusty water onto the tall weeds. Darting in and out from under the trucks was a flock of squawking long-necked geese. Through this maze I could see a garage door and assumed correctly that the house must be attached to the garage, or rather, to be more accurate, there was a long workshop attached to the garage and the house was attached to the workshop. I headed down a narrow path flanked with stacks of lobster traps, where cats and kittens played with the ropes and lines and gnawed on the nets. Near the end of the path I was greeted by two hand-made signs. One read: "Beware Of Dogs - No Trespassing," and the other read: "Antiques Made To Order."

When I found the front door, which was on the side of this rustic building complex, across from a bunkhouse, which Linc built, I knocked, but got no immediate response. I was nervous about the dog sign; and the side yard, which looked like a jungle with corn stocks and goldenrod growing up to the doorstop, didn't help to calm my nerves. Then I heard a grunt from behind the garden, high up on a rocky hill. Looking up I saw the silhouette of a horse standing on the rocks. How the horse got up there, or why it was there, I didn't know, but I concluded it had to be just another of Linc's many pets. Growls and barking from more than one dog came from within the house, and I seriously considered dropping the bag of food by the door and heading home.

"Who is it?" a gruff, raspy voice finally inquired from within. "Bob Cahill with Henryetta's dinner," I replied. "Well, what the hell you doin' at this door?" Linc snarled in his distinctive Marblehead drawl. "Go round to the gay-rage door and I'll let ya in, otherwise, the dogs'll chew ya to pieces." I obeyed and Linc, wearing overalls, plaid shirt and cap, with eyeglasses hanging from his broad nose, was there to greet me. He squinted over his glasses at the bag I was carrying. "What ya got for her?" he asked. "I have no idea." I replied. "Kenny just asked me to deliver it." Linc grunted approvingly, as I felt something peck at my ankle. It was a chicken. Linc booted it out of the way and led me into a dark room off the garage. The room was filled with work benches and tools, with a large anvil sitting in the middle of the floor. Much like a blacksmith shop of the 1800's might look, I thought, but the smell in the room was almost unbearable. Linc saw my nostrils twitch. "Don't mind the smell," he chuckled, "that's Henryetta." He led me across the room to a stall and opened the door, motioning me inside. "Just dump the food in there," he said matter of factly. In the shadows of the stall I could see a large white beast, staring at me with beady red eyes — it was a hog, the largest I had ever seen. No one had told me that Henryetta was a hog!

"Go ahead in and give her the food," ordered Linc. I hesitated. I could see a large fang sticking out from under her snout. "She doesn't bite, does she?" "Hell no," said Linc, sounding impatient. "She ain't bit anyone I know." I entered the pen to dump the food, which I now realized was garbage from Maddie's, but missed the trough completely. Henryetta darted from the shadows and headed straight at me. I lifted my foot for protection, spilling the garbage all over me. She clamped down on my shoe with her sharp teeth — I could feel the pain on my toes. I kicked and struggled, trying to make my way back out of the stall, but Henryetta wouldn't let go. I looked over at Linc for help, but he was just leaning on the stall shaking his head. When I got to the stall door, I let out a holler and pulled as hard as I could to free my foot. Henryetta reluctantly let go and I slammed the stall door on her snout. Her teeth had actually broken through the shoe leather, but hadn't broken the skin. My toes, however, throbbed with pain — I was furious.

"I thought you said she didn't bite?" I shouted at Linc, who stared at me with an impish grin. "Well hell," he said, "she ain't never done that before, not to a Marbleheader anyway . . . Couldn't be that you ain't from these parts, could it? . . . I mean, you ain't an outsider are you?" "I'm not a Yankee, if that's what you mean," I shouted at him angrily. "I'm Irish, from Salem." "Well, that's it then, boy," said Linc in all seriousness, stroking the silver whiskers on his chin. "Henryetta has been cravin some of that Irish blood for months now. It ain't that she don't like Irishmen, it's just 'cause their blood has so much whiskey in it, I suppose . . . Hell for a minute there I thought poor Henryetta had gone out of her mind. I don't like to see her get all excited like that . . . Kenny Duncan should've known better. When you see him, you tell him to send up some pure blooded Yankee lad with her supper next time." Linc patted me on the back and kept shaking his head as he saw me to the door. As I limped home, I was sure that the moment I left Linc's side, he was on the phone to Kenny Duncan and the two of them had a good laugh.

Two months passed before I saw Henryetta again. She was steaming hot and smelling good — I indulged with great gusto. The menu board at Maddie's read: "Henryetta - roast, with potatoes and corn - $3.95 - porkchops with all the fixings - $2.95."

It was only a few years before my misadventure with Linc and Henryetta, that almost the entire town of Marblehead showed up at Redd's Pond one wintry morning to see Linc perform a miracle. He had been given $500 to tear down and old red barn located across Redd's Pond from his own property. Instead of tearing it down, Linc decided to transport the barn in one piece across the pond to his side. He could make $500 and get a barn for himself in the process. Most of the Townies didn't think he could do it, which only made Linc all the more determined that he would. In February, the ice on the pond was about one-foot thick, strong enough — Linc concluded — to allow him to just slide the barn across to his side, no more than 100 yards away. Linc and his two helpers managed to get the barn onto the ice, but then came three warm days, during which time the ice began to melt. The gathered town folks laughed as Linc was quickly forced to place the barn back to where he had moved it from, and Linc didn't like that.

Next day, the Salem Evening News headlined: "Journeys End For The Big Red Barn," and a tongue-in-cheek article on Lincoln Hawkes' folly followed the headline. Linc was angry. He called the newspaper. "You shouldn't have written that article," he shouted at the editor. "I'm not going to have to tear that barn down. In fact, I'm going to get it across the pond in one piece. I'm going to row it across with a Grand Banks dory."

In town, Ambrose Brown started taking bets, 5 to 1, that Linc couldn't do it. One of Linc's cousins reported that, "Lincoln has no education and doesn't understand the center of gravity. It's obvious that the barn will either tip over or sink." Linc got some heavy timbers, 120 oil drums, and he built a raft to set the barn on. With hundreds watching, on the day the ice disappeared from the pond, he and his pal Jerry Smith slipped a Grand Banks dory into the pond, hitched it to the raft, and started rowing. When the barn was half way across the pond, Linc stood up in the boat, bowed to the cheering crowd, then took a pint of Old Thomson whiskey from under his overalls and swigged it down. Then he shouted to his outspoken cousin who was watching the proceedings from the opposite bank. "Well, cousin," he yelled across the water, "I may not be educated, but you've got just enough education to be dangerous." The crowd roared their approval and Linc rowed on until the barn was safely landed on the opposite shore, where it remains to this day. "Hell,

I could have rowed that barn 100 miles down the Mississippi River," he told the news reporter. Most Marbleheaders learned a lesson that day; you just don't tell Linc Hawkes that he can't do something.

A few years later, the Marblehead Police made that same mistake. Linc drives an old maroon convertible that he's owned for years: but as Linc himself will admit, he's not one of the best drivers in town. One day the police took away his license. Linc put up no fuss. He merely brought out an old hay wagon he had stored in the yard, and hitched two of his horses up to it — and that's how he travelled around town until he got his license back. To get even with the police though, he found an old ordinance in the town records, one that the selectmen had forgotten to take off the books. It read that, "Old Town Hall in Town Square (where the police station was located) is to forever be a watering place for horses." Linc drove his big noisy wagon down the narrow streets and halted in front of the police station, immediately creating a traffic jam. The angry police ordered Linc to move on. He refused, then he read aloud the ordinance. A large crowd began to gather. "You must give my horses water," he shouted. "It's the law." "Can we pull him in for drunk horse driving? one confused policeman inquired of another.

"I demand water," Linc insisted, and now some of the crowd began to echo Linc's demand. Two policemen scurried into the station, found two buckets, filled them with water and ran back out to the street to feed the horses. "Yes sir," Linc addressed the crowd as the horses drank, "the police have to obey our laws too." The police then escorted Linc and his horse and wagon back home. Later, the police found another more recent ordinance which forbid horses to be ridden through town except during parades. Linc retaliated with a scathing editorial in the newspaper, stating that horses have as much right in town as people. "Strong horses and strong men built this country," said Linc. "If a horse leaves something on the road, nature will take care of it . . . Little sparrows have to eat too," he concluded.

Linc has always had one or two horses coralled in his rocky backyard, and recently, he had a donkey and a bull there as well. The donkey was a birthday present to Linc's pal Vance Smith, but Smith had Linc care for it. The bull came from no one knows where, and all that Linc will say is that. "I carried him home in my arms, saving him from the slaughter house." As the bull grew up, he repeatedly broke loose from the confines of Linc's yard to raid neighboring gardens, and the donkey would always follow. They were an inseparable pair and a sight to behold, tearing down the streets of Marblehead, striking fear into visiting tourists, with the police usually close on their tails.

On Election Day, 1983, Linc left the donkey at home, and strolled into town with the bull in tow. Displayed over the back of the bull like a riding blanket was one of Linc's homemade signs, which read: "Vote Today For Nobody." His first stop was the local china shop, but he only allowed the bull to stick his head in the door, enough to frighten the shop owner. Then Linc led the bull down State Street to Maddie's Sail Loft, with a great procession of people following. Linc wanted to surprise Kenny Duncan by bringing the bull into the bar, but he wouldn't fit through the door. Linc strolled on toward the waterfront, until he and the bull reached another favorite Marblehead watering hole called The Landing. The bull fit through The Landing's swinging doors. It was Linda the bartender's first day on the job. She screamed, then ordered Linc to, "get out of here with that beast."

"I will," said Linc, tying the bull to the brass rail, "but first I must have a taste." Linc sat on a barstool, while Linda nervously and quickly served him. The bull was noticeably nervous too, for the bar was filling with curious tourists and Townies. The bull then answered nature's call on the barroom floor. Linda screamed again and the crowd went into hysterics. "Don't get excited," cautioned Linc, getting up from the barstool to kick the droppings out the door.

"Somebody called the cops," a friend whispered into Linc's ear. Linc quickly unhitched the bull and dragged him out the door, then towed him down a back street towards home. The police showed up at Linc's house later — he was forced to finally sell the bull to a slaughter house.

Linc's favorite animal is a rooster that parades among the horses, dogs, cats, geese, and pigs, like it's king of the roost. When I visit Linc, I often find him in his rocking chair in the back room, with the rooster on his lap. Linc will pet it and sing it lullabies, rocking it gently until it falls asleep.

Linc Hawkes is the last of the Grand Old Yankees, the kind who demanded then won their independence from Mother England in the 18th Century. Marbleheaders will be the first to tell you, "there's nothing Linc can't do, and there's nothing Linc won't do." He's a master mechanic, carpenter, rigger, talented musician and poet, and most of the food he eats he either gathers from the sea or produces himself in his own backyard, In a town full of interesting and unique people, Lincoln Hawkes is Marblehead's most gifted and unusual character — to me, he is a very special man of wit and wisdom, one of the finest and funniest men I have met.